THE LOS ANGELES KINGS

KURT WALDENDORF

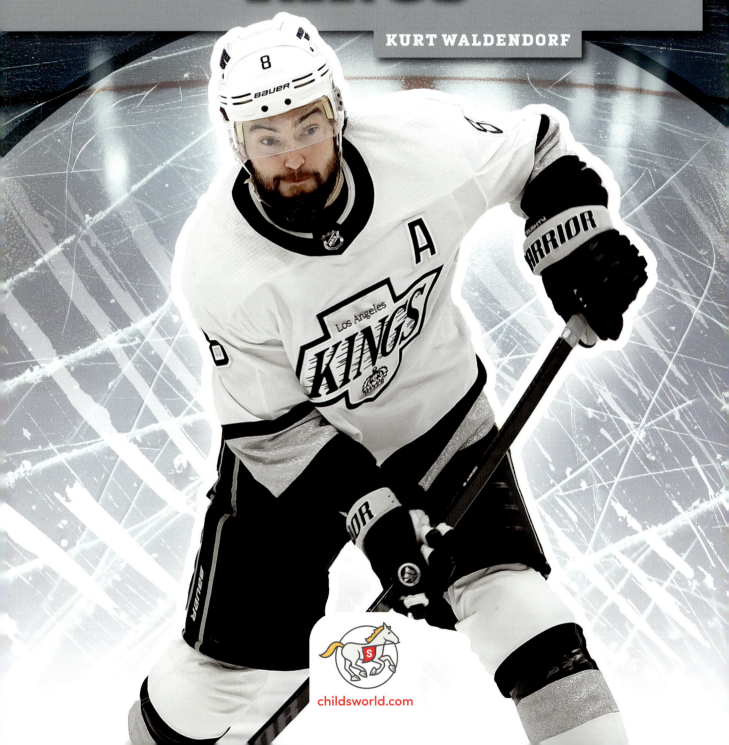

childsworld.com

Published by The Child's World®
800-599-READ • www.childsworld.com

Copyright © 2026 by The Child's World®
All rights reserved. No part of this book may be reproduced or utilized in any form or by any means without written permission from the publisher.

Photography Credits
Cover: ©Andy Devlin/NHLI/Getty Images; multiple pages: ©Hanna Siamashka/iStock/Getty Images; GLYPHstock/iStock/Getty Images; md tauhidul/Shutterstock; page 5: ©Harry How/Getty Images; page 6: ©Denis Brodeur/NHLI/Getty Images; page 9: ©Bruce Bennett/Getty Images; page 10: ©Jakub Porzycki/NurPhoto/Getty Images; page 12: ©Gary A. Vasquez/NHLI/Getty Images; page 12: ©Chris Tanouye/Freestyle Photography/Getty Images; page 13: ©Art Foxall/Bruce Bennett/Getty Images; page 13: ©W Roberts/Bruce Bennett Studios via Getty Images Studios/Getty Images; page 14: ©Adam Pantozzi/NHLI/Getty Images; page 16: ©Steve Babineau/NHLI/Getty Images; page 16: ©Focus on Sport/Getty Images; page 17: ©Kellie Landis/Allsport/Getty Images; page 17: ©Juan Ocampo/NHLI/Getty Images; page 18: ©Bruce Bennett Studios via Getty Images Studios/Getty Images; page 18: ©Bruce Bennett Studios via Getty Images Studios/Getty Images; page 19: ©Dave Sandford/NHLI/Getty Images for NHL/Getty Images; page 19: ©Robert Gauthier/Los Angeles Times/Getty Images: page 20: ©Juan Ocampo/NHLI/Getty Images; page 20: ©Gary A. Vasquez/NHLI/Getty Images; page 21: ©Ronald Martinez/Getty Images; page 21: ©Will Navarro/NHLI/Getty Images; page 22: ©Bruce Bennett Studios via Getty Images Studios/Getty Images; page 23: ©Steve Babineau/NHLI/Getty Images; page 25: ©Bruce Bennett/Getty Images; page 26: ©Jonathan Daniel/Getty Images; page 29: ©Andy Devlin/NHLI/Getty Images

ISBN Information
9781503870758 (Reinforced Library Binding)
9781503871915 (Portable Document Format)
9781503873155 (Online Multi-user eBook)
9781503874398 (Electronic Publication)

LCCN
Library of Congress Control Number: 2024950247

Printed in the United States of America

ABOUT THE AUTHOR

Kurt Waldendorf is the author of more than a dozen books for children. When he's not writing or editing, he enjoys indoor rock climbing and running along the shore of Lake Michigan with his dog. He lives in Chicago.

CONTENTS

Go Kings! . . . 4
Becoming the Kings . . . 7
By the Numbers . . . 8
Game Night . . . 11
Uniforms . . . 12
Team Spirit . . . 15
Heroes of History . . . 16
Big Days . . . 18
Modern-Day Marvels . . . 20
The G.O.A.T. . . . 23
The Big Game . . . 24
Amazing Feats . . . 27
All-Time Best . . . 28

Glossary...30
Fast Facts...31
One Stride Further...31
Find Out More...32
Index...32

Go Kings!

The Los Angeles Kings compete in the National Hockey League's (NHL) Western Conference. They play in the Pacific **Division** with the Anaheim Ducks, Calgary Flames, Edmonton Oilers, San Jose Sharks, Seattle Kraken, Vancouver Canucks, and Vegas Golden Knights. The Kings have played in the NHL for more than 50 seasons. The team has appeared in the **playoffs** in 33 seasons. The team has won two Stanley Cups. Let's learn more about the Kings.

Western Conference • Pacific Division

Anaheim Ducks	Edmonton Oilers	San Jose Sharks	Vancouver Canucks
Calgary Flames	Los Angeles Kings	Seattle Kraken	Vegas Golden Knights

Kings players celebrate a win over the Pittsburgh Penguins during the 2022–2023 season.

Goalie Rogie Vachon (center) played seven of his 16 NHL seasons in LA. He returned to the Kings as an assistant coach in 1983.

Becoming the Kings

In 1967, the NHL went from six teams to 12. One of the new teams was the Los Angeles Kings. The team had a tough start but found success in the 1970s. Led by center Marcel Dionne, they made it to the playoffs nine times in a row. Then in 1988, the Kings made one of the biggest trades in hockey history. Wayne Gretzky arrived from the Edmonton Oilers. Gretzky was the best player in the league. He helped lead the Kings to their first Stanley Cup Final in 1993. But the team lost to the Montreal Canadiens. After trading Gretzky to another team in the late 1990s, the team went through another tough stretch. In 2012, the team finally broke through. Goaltender Jonathan Quick and defenseman Drew Doughty led the team to its first title. Two years later, they won a second. In recent years, experienced players from those title teams have been joined by a promising young group of players. The future is bright for the Kings.

By the Numbers

he Kings have had a lot of success on the ice. Here are just a few interesting facts:

 The Kings have won the Stanley Cup two times, in 2012 and 2014. **2**

 The team has ranked first in their division once in team history. **1**

 The most wins by a Kings team was 48 in 2015–2016. **48**

 The Kings have reached the NHL playoffs 33 times. **33**

Although they made it to the playoffs several times, the Kings played their first 45 seasons without a Stanley Cup title.

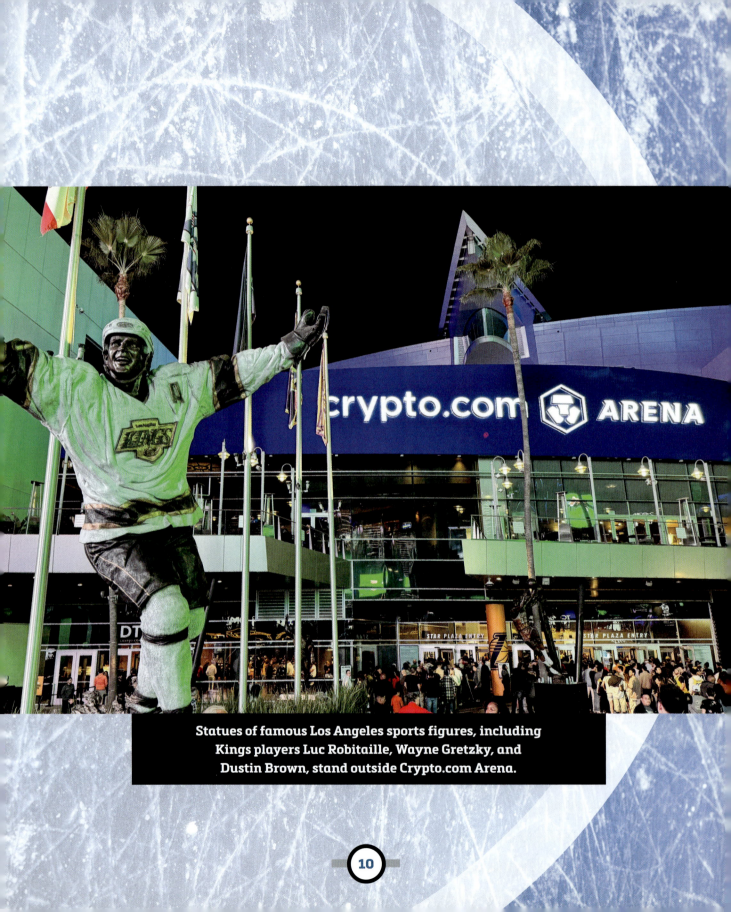

Statues of famous Los Angeles sports figures, including Kings players Luc Robitaille, Wayne Gretzky, and Dustin Brown, stand outside Crypto.com Arena.

Game Night

For 30 years, the Kings played in the Forum. It was one of the most famous stadiums in the country. It was made to look like the Colosseum from ancient Rome. In 1999, the Staples Center opened. In 2021, its name changed to Crypto.com Arena. The building is home to the Kings as well as the Los Angeles Lakers of the National Basketball Association and the Los Angeles Sparks of the Women's National Basketball Association. The arena also hosts concerts and other events, such as the GRAMMY Awards. In all, about four million people visit Crypto.com Arena each year.

We're Famous!

Los Angeles is home to many famous athletes, actors, and musicians. As a result, the Kings have some of the league's most famous fans. Musician Snoop Dogg and actor Will Ferrell are big Kings fans. Other celebrities, such as Taylor Swift, Katy Perry, Tom Hanks, Elliot Page, and Zac Efron, have also been spotted in the stands. Over the years, actors such as Cuba Gooding Jr. have played in Kings celebrity hockey games to raise money for charity.

Uniforms

HOME

AWAY

Goalie Gear

Goalie masks don't just protect players from the puck. They also give players a place to show pride in their team and city. Kings goalies have often represented their royal nickname by including crowns on their helmets. Stéphane Fiset included a different king-like figure. His "King Tut" mask showed a headdress of a leader from ancient Egypt. Other goalies have honored their city. Kelly Hrudey's "Hollywood" mask showed the Los Angeles Hollywood Hills sign. The sign is a symbol of the city's entertainment industry.

Truly Weird

The Kings' jerseys have gone through lots of changes over time. In 1988, the team successfully updated its colors from purple and gold to black and silver. The team had just traded for Wayne Gretzky. The change represented an exciting new period for the Kings. In 1995, the team made a less popular change. It introduced a logo that showed a king's head with a purple beard. Fans jokingly called it the "Burger King" logo. The team stopped using the logo after one season.

Team Spirit

Los Angeles Kings fans are passionate about their team. At each game, almost 18,000 fans cheer on their squad. Bailey the Lion has been the team's mascot since 2007. Lions represent strength and royalty, just like the team's nickname. Bailey bangs on a drum and leads the fans in "Go Kings Go!" chants. The team's drumline helps fire up the crowd. The Anaheim Ducks are the Kings' biggest **rival**. Games between the two are called "Freeway Face-Offs." The teams' stadiums are connected by California's Highway 5. The Kings also have a rivalry with the Edmonton Oilers because of the Wayne Gretzky trade. The Kings and Oilers faced off in the 2022, 2023, and 2024 playoffs.

◀ When Bailey the Lion is not helping fans get hyped up during home games, he is visiting schools and hospitals in the Los Angeles area.

Heroes of History

Wayne Gretzky
Center | 1988–1996

The player called "The Great One" is best-known for his time with the Edmonton Oilers. But a big part of Wayne Gretzky's legend was built in Southern California. The Gretzky trade made the Kings the most talked-about team in the NHL. On the ice, Gretzky lived up to the talk. During his first season with the Kings, he scored 54 goals and was named the league's most valuable player (MVP). Across eight seasons with the Kings, he averaged an amazing 1.7 points per game. Gretzky remains among the team leaders in points and assists.

Luc Robitaille
Left Winger | 1986–1994, 1997–2001, 2003–2006

When the Kings picked Luc Robitaille 171st in the 1984 NHL Draft, fans did not expect much. But he would become one of the best players of his time. While Robitaille wasn't the best skater, he was a natural goal scorer. In his first season, he notched 45 goals. He was named Rookie of the Year. He went on to set the record for most goals by a Kings player, with 557. After he retired, Robitaille was named to the Hall of Fame. And in 2017, he was named Kings team president.

Rob Blake
Defenseman | 1989–2001, 2006–2008

Rob Blake was among the NHL's most feared players in the 1990s. On defense, he was big and physical. On offense, he was a skilled scorer. In 1993, Blake and Gretzky led the Kings to the Stanley Cup Final. When Gretzky was traded away in 1996, Blake took over as captain. Two years later, he won the Norris Trophy as the top defenseman in the league. Blake never won a Stanley Cup as a Kings player. But he was part of the Kings' 2014 title run as assistant general manager. In 2017, Blake became the Kings' general manager.

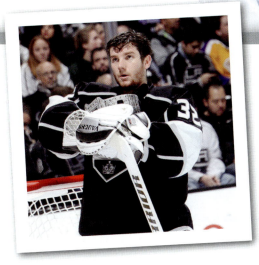

Jonathan Quick
Goaltender | 2007–2023

No player did more to bring a Stanley Cup to Los Angeles than Jonathan Quick. In the 2012 playoffs, Quick went on an amazing run. In 20 playoff games, he never allowed more than three goals per game. He led the NHL in save percentage. His efforts earned him a playoff MVP trophy and the first of two Stanley Cup titles. Across 16 seasons with the Kings, Quick racked up more than 18,000 saves and 57 shutouts, by far the most for any Kings goalie.

Big Days

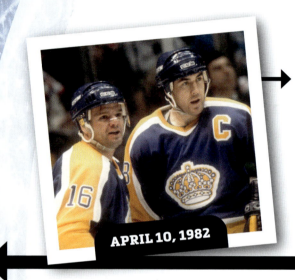

APRIL 10, 1982

After trailing the Edmonton Oilers 5–0, the Kings come back to win 6–5 in a first-round playoff game. The amazing comeback is known as the "Miracle on Manchester" because of the Forum's address.

The Kings send three top draft picks, two players, and $15 million to the Edmonton Oilers for Wayne Gretzky and two other players. The trade brings new popularity to the team.

AUGUST 9, 1988

JUNE 11, 2012

The Kings win their first Stanley Cup title, beating the New Jersey Devils four games to two. It is the team's first title since coming into the league in 1967.

The Kings beat the New York Rangers to win the series four games to one and claim their second title. Kings defenseman Alec Martinez scores the winning goal in the second **overtime** period.

JUNE 13, 2014

Modern-Day Marvels

Anže Kopitar
Center | 2006–Present

In 2006, Anže Kopitar became the first player from the country of Slovenia to play in the NHL. Since then, he's made a name for himself as a top center in the league. In the 2012 and 2014 playoffs, he led the league in points, bringing the Kings to titles in each season. He also shines at the other end of the rink. Kopitar has twice won the Selke Trophy, which is given to the center or winger who is most skilled on defense. Kopitar is a five-time All-Star and team captain.

Drew Doughty
Defenseman | 2008–Present

Since earning a spot on the Kings at age 18, defenseman Drew Doughty has been a star. In 2009, he was named to the All-Rookie team. In 2012 and 2014, his impressive defense and skilled scoring helped lead the Kings to their Stanley Cup titles. In 2016, Doughty received the Norris Trophy, given to the league's top defenseman. Doughty dealt with a knee injury in 2021 and an ankle injury in 2024. But when he's on the ice, he remains a team leader and top defenseman.

Adrian Kempe
Right Winger | 2016–Present

Alongside veterans such as Kopitar and Doughty, the Kings have a promising group of young players. One is Swedish winger Adrian Kempe. Since playing his first full season in 2017–2018, the speedy Swede has continued to improve. In 2022, he was selected for his first All-Star game. And in 2024, Kempe notched a career-high 75 points to lead the team. As he takes on an even bigger role, the future looks bright for the young star.

Quinton Byfield
Center | 2021–Present

Another promising young player is Canadian Quinton Byfield. The second pick in the 2020 NHL Draft has all the tools to be a star. He's big, strong, fast, and skilled. After dealing with injuries in his first seasons with the Kings, Byfield found his stride in 2024, scoring 55 points in 80 games. The team hopes that as Kopitar nears the end of his career, the promising Byfield will be ready to take the spot as the top center on the team.

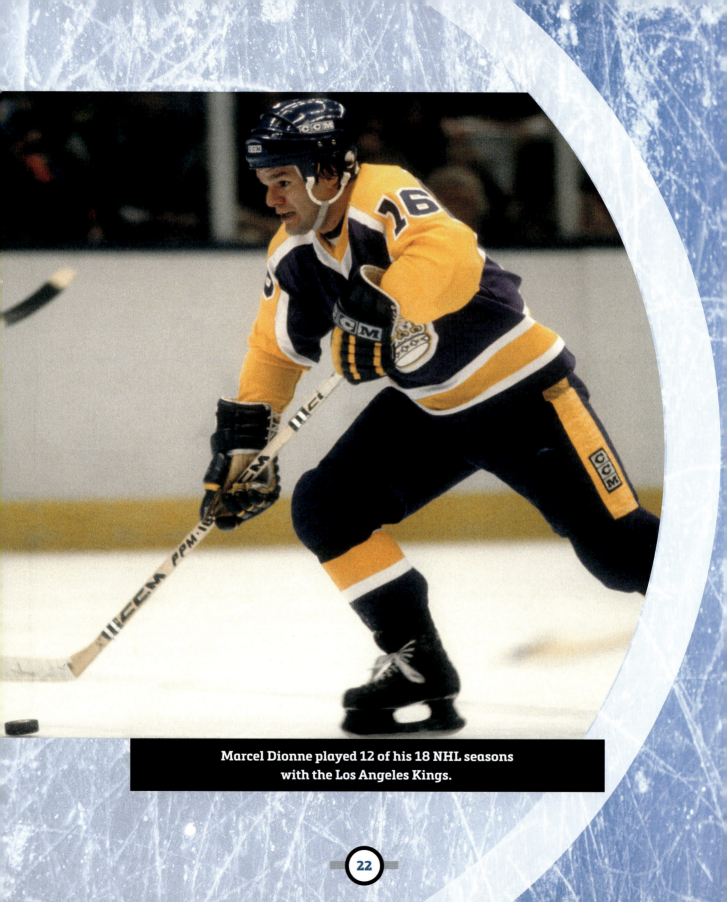
Marcel Dionne played 12 of his 18 NHL seasons with the Los Angeles Kings.

The G.O.A.T.

The best-ever Kings career belongs to Marcel Dionne. Drafted in 1971, the small, speedy Dionne was a world-class scorer. From 1975 to 1978, he was selected to four-straight All-Star games. In 1979, he was placed on a **line** with winger Dave Taylor and center Charlie Simmer. The "Triple Crown" line became the most feared in the league. Dionne led the NHL with 137 points. While Dionne never won a Stanley Cup, he was twice voted the most outstanding player by NHL players. His 731 goals rank sixth all-time. In 1992, Dionne was selected for the Hockey Hall of Fame.

Fan Favorite

At just 5 feet, 7 inches (1.7 m) tall, Rogatien "Rogie" Vachon was small for a goalie. He made up for it with a quick glove and athletic moves. In 1975, Vachon became the first Kings player to have his jersey retired. Years later, he finally got the credit he deserved from the hockey world. Vachon was selected to the Hockey Hall of Fame in 2016.

The Big Game

The 2012 Kings were not expected to do well in the playoffs. They were the eighth **seed**. That meant they had to play the best teams in the conference to reach the Stanley Cup Final. But the top teams were no match for the Kings. They defeated the Vancouver Canucks in five games. Then, they beat the St. Louis Blues in four games and the Phoenix Coyotes in five. In the Stanley Cup Final, the Kings jumped out to a three-game lead over the New Jersey Devils. They then lost two games straight. Just as it looked like the Kings' run might come to an end, the team's offense exploded. In Game 6, they scored six goals. Goaltender Jonathan Quick let in just one from the Devils. As Kings captain Dustin Brown raised the Stanley Cup trophy, Kings great Luc Robitaille, then part of the Kings' staff, joined the team on the ice. Together, they celebrated the team's first title.

The Kings finished the 2011–2012 season third in their division, but they went on to win the first Stanley Cup in team history.

Jonathan Quick spent 16 seasons with the Kings and made more than 18,100 saves for the team.

Amazing Feats

Shutouts
In 69 games in the 2011–2012 season, Jonathan Quick recorded 10 shutouts. Quick went on to be named playoff MVP as the Kings won their first title.

10

Penalty Minutes
With Wayne Gretzky on the team, defenseman Marty McSorley's role was to protect the team's star. In the 1992–1993 season, McSorley racked up 399 penalty minutes in 81 games.

399

Defenseman Points
In his rookie season, defenseman Larry Murphy scored 16 goals and had 60 assists for a total of 76 points. Murphy went on to a 21-year Hall of Fame career.

76

Power Play Goals
Playing alongside Wayne Gretzky in 1991–1992, Luc Robitaille scored a team record 26 **power play** goals.

26

All-Time Best

MOST POINTS
1	Marcel Dionne	1,307
2	Anže Kopitar*	1,250
3	Luc Robitaille	1,154
4	Dave Taylor	1,069
5	Wayne Gretzky	918

MOST GOALS
1	Luc Robitaille	557
2	Marcel Dionne	550
3	Dave Taylor	431
	Anže Kopitar*	431
5	Bernie Nicholls	327

MOST ASSISTS
1	Anže Kopitar*	819
2	Marcel Dionne	757
3	Wayne Gretzky	672
4	Dave Taylor	638
5	Luc Robitaille	597

HAT TRICKS
1	Marcel Dionne	24
2	Bernie Nicholls	14
3	Luc Robitaille	14
4	Butch Goring	10
5	Dave Taylor	8

SAVES
1	Jonathan Quick	18,188
2	Kelly Hrudey	10,151
3	Rogie Vachon	9,967
4	Mario Lessard	5,870
5	Stéphane Fiset	5,160

SHUTOUTS
1	Jonathan Quick	57
2	Rogie Vachon	32
3	Jamie Storr	16
4	Félix Potvin	14
5	Stéphane Fiset	10
	Kelly Hrudey	10

*stats accurate through December 2024

Anže Kopitar earned 1,211 points, including 419 goals, in his first 18 seasons with the Kings.

GLOSSARY

division (dih-VIZSH-un) A division is a group of teams within the NHL that compete with each other to have the best record each season and advance to the playoffs.

draft (DRAFT) A draft is a yearly event when teams take turns choosing new players. In the NHL, teams can select North American ice hockey players between the ages of 18 and 20 and international players between 18 and 21 to join the league.

line (LYN) A line in hockey is made up of a center, left winger, and right winger who are on the ice at the same time.

overtime (OH-vur-tym) Overtime is extra time added to the end of a game when the regular time is up and the score is tied.

playoffs (PLAY-offs) Playoffs are games that take place after the end of the regular season to determine each year's championship team.

power play (POW-uhr PLAY) A power play occurs when a player gets a penalty and the other team has more players on the ice.

rival (RYE-vuhl) A rival is a team's top competitor, which they try to outdo and play better than each season.

rookie (ROOK-ee) A rookie is a new or first-year player in a professional sport.

save percentage (SAYV per-SEN-tij) Save percentage is a measure of how often a goalie blocks a shot from going into the goal.

seed (SEED) A seed is a team's ranking going into a tournament.

shutout (SHUT-owt) A shutout occurs when a goalie keeps the other team from scoring any goals.

FAST FACTS

- The original colors of the Los Angeles Kings were purple and gold to match the Los Angeles Lakers basketball team. The teams shared the same owner.

- Because of the success of the Gretzky trade, the NHL expanded to other warm US cities. Two more teams came to California, and two teams were introduced in Florida.

- In 2012, the Kings became the first team in any major US sport to win a title as an eighth seed.

- In October 2023, Anže Kopitar became the all-time leader in games played for the Kings, passing Dustin Brown's mark of 1,296.

ONE STRIDE FURTHER

- Luc Robitaille scored more than 100 points in four separate seasons with the Kings. Wayne Gretzky holds the single-season record for points with 168. Which accomplishment do you think is more impressive and why?

- Based on what you've learned from this book, what do you think it takes for a team to win the Stanley Cup? Is it great scoring? Excellent defenders? A top goalie? What about leadership? Discuss your opinion with a friend.

- Players around the world train hard to make it to the NHL. Write a paragraph describing the skills and attitudes you think it takes to reach the highest level.

- Ask friends and family members to name their favorite sport to watch and their favorite sport to play. Keep track and make a graph to see which sports are the most popular.

FIND OUT MORE

IN THE LIBRARY

Anderson, Josh. *G.O.A.T. Hockey Goalies*. Minneapolis, MN: Lerner, 2024.

Graves, Will. *Pro Hockey Upsets*. Minneapolis, MN: Lerner, 2020.

Laughlin, Kara L. *Hockey*. Parker, CO: The Child's World, 2024.

Walker, Tracy Sue. *Wayne Gretzky: The Great One*. Minneapolis, MN: Lerner, 2023.

ON THE WEB

Visit our website for links about the Los Angeles Kings:
childsworld.com/links

Note to Parents, Caregivers, Teachers, and Librarians: We routinely verify our web links to make sure they are safe and active sites. So encourage your readers to check them out!

INDEX

Bailey the Lion 15
Blake, Rob 17
Byfield, Quinton 21

Crypto.com Arena 10–11

Dionne, Marcel 7, 22–23, 28
Doughty, Drew 7, 20–21

Gretzky, Wayne 7, 10, 13, 15–18, 27–28, 31

Kempe, Adrian 21
Kopitar, Anže 20–21, 28, 31

Pacific Division 4

Quick, Jonathan 7, 17, 24, 26–28

Robitaille, Luc 10, 16, 24, 27–28, 31

Stanley Cup 4, 7–8, 17, 19–20, 23–24, 31

Vachon, Rogatien 6, 23, 28